THE LORD IS MY SHEPHERD

THE LORD IS MY SHEPHERD

Reflections on

God's Loving Care

A D R I A N   R O G E R S

C R O S S W A Y   B O O K S ,   W H E A T O N ,   I L L I N O I S
A   D I V I S I O N   O F   G O O D   N E W S   P U B L I S H E R S

The Lord Is My Shepherd

Copyright ©1999 by Adrian Rogers

Published by Crossway Books
          A division of Good News Publishers
          1300 Crescent Street
          Wheaton, Illinois 60187

Unless otherwise indicated, Scripture quotations are taken from the *King James Version.*

Verses marked NIV are taken from the *New International Version.*

Cover design: David LaPlaca

Illustrations: Debra Chabrian

First printing, new edition 2003

Printed in China

LIBRARY OF CONGRESS CATALOGING-IN-PUBLICATION DATA

Rogers, Adrian.
The Lord is my shepherd : reflections on God's loving care / Adrian Rogers.
      p. cm.
ISBN 1-58134-575-5 (hardcover : alk. paper)
1. Bible. O.T. Psalms XXIII--Devotional literature. I. Title.
BS1450 23rd.R64 1999
242'.5--dc21   98-51509

IM		13	12	11	10	09	08	07	06	05	04	03
15	14	13	12	11	10	9	8	7	6	5	4	3	2	1

DEDICATION

This work is gratefully dedicated to the staff and volunteer workers of Love Worth Finding Ministries. Thank you each one for holding up my hands and being partners in getting out the Gospel. "The Lord gave the word: great was the company of those that published it." Psalm 68:11

ACKNOWLEDGMENTS

I want to thank my co-workers and friends whose encouragement helped to bring this book into being.

I especially wish to thank Julia Flanagan for her invaluable help in editorial work and for creative material that she has supplied.

I am also grateful to the good people at Crossway Books. I love and admire the President of Crossway, Lane Dennis, and am grateful for his guidance and patience with me.

To God be glory both now and forever.
Adrian Rogers

CONTENTS

1 The Shepherd We Need   11

2 The Perfect Shepherd   27

3 The Shepherd of the Second Chance   43

4 The Shepherd of the Dying   61

5 The Shepherd of Plenty   77

6 The Shepherd of Heaven   95

Psalm 23

The LORD is my shepherd; I shall not want.

He maketh me to lie down in green pastures;

He leadeth me beside the still waters.

He restoreth my soul;

He leadeth me in the paths of righteousness for his name's sake.

Yea, though I walk through the valley of the shadow of death, I will fear no evil;

For thou art with me; thy rod and thy staff they comfort me.

Thou preparest a table before me in the presence of mine enemies;

Thou anointest my head with oil; my cup runneth over.

Surely goodness and mercy shall follow me all the days of my life;

And I will dwell in the house of the LORD for ever.

CHAPTER ONE

THE SHEPHERD WE NEED

All my life long I had panted

For a drink from some cool spring

That I hoped would quench the burning

Of the thirst I felt within.

Feeding on the food around me

'Til my strength was almost gone,

Longed my soul for something better,

Only still to hunger on.

CLARA T. WILLIAMS

~&

*P*salm 23 is one of the most beloved passages of Scripture of all time the world over. Its beautiful lines feed our souls beyond ways we understand. A Shepherd who loves us and provides all that we need—we all yearn for that, don't we? In this world of conflict and challenge and need, having hearts that long for something higher and deeper, we are looking for a heart-contentment that we know we can't provide for ourselves.

THE SEARCH FOR SATISFACTION

How many truly satisfied people do you know? By that, I don't mean they never struggle, never hurt. But they have reached a place in their lives where they can say, as Paul said, "I have learned, in whatsoever state I am, therewith to be content" (Philippians 4:11).

Of course, part of the journey in discovering the secret to satisfaction is in defining the term. What satisfies one person may not satisfy another. I enjoy great satisfaction when my entire family gets together. For others, a family get-together could provide just the opposite effect—stress! We all define and achieve satisfaction in different ways.

The Scottish-born naturalist and founder of the Sierra Club, John Muir, once had a conversation with railroad magnate and industrialist E. H. Harriman. "I am richer than you are," declared Muir to the railroad baron. "And how is that true?" responded Harriman. "Because you don't have all you want—and I do. Therefore I am richer than you," answered Muir.

Perhaps these two men were playing word games with one another. We don't know if either man was truly satisfied with his life. But one thing I'm sure of—our search for satisfaction will not be found at the end of a rainbow in a pot of gold. I agree with the author of Ecclesiastes on this point: "He that loveth silver shall not be satisfied with silver; nor he that loveth abundance with increase: this is also vanity" (Ecclesiastes 5:10).

I heard a story about a little boy that well illustrated this point. He loved pancakes so much that he sometimes made a glutton of himself. His mother thought she would cure him of this, so one day she offered to cook all the pancakes he could eat. She made them. He ate them. She made more. He ate more. When she was about to pour another ladle full of batter onto the hot griddle, she asked him, "Son, do you want another pancake?" He groaned, "No, ma'am. In fact, I don't want the ones I've already had."

Where are you looking for satisfaction? How will you know when you've found it? And when you think you've discovered the secret of satisfaction, will it last for eternity?

In the deepest recesses of our hearts and minds, there are hungers that cannot be satisfied by the things of this world. St. Augustine once said that we were created with a God-shaped void. I agree. Only God can meet the deepest longings of our hearts. Nothing can satisfy us apart from a personal relationship with Him.

This is not because He is a heavy-handed dictator forcing us to accept life the way He dishes it out, but because He knows and loves us. Who knows what will satisfy your deepest needs better than the One who made you? As your Creator, He can see what your needs are going to be tomorrow and ten years from tomorrow. So He certainly knows what you need today!

THE SECRET OF SATISFACTION

Every word in the Bible is a precious and sacred jewel. Never is that more true than in the crown jewels of Psalm 23.

Let your mind simply rest on the words "The LORD" in this verse. What comes to your mind? When David wrote this Psalm, he was thinking there was one God. Most ancient cultures had scores, if not hundreds, of gods. From the very beginning David wanted to make it crystal-clear to his readers that the Lord is the one and only God. Many other images may come to your mind, but I want you to think of the sovereign God. *Sovereign* means supreme. "The LORD" of Psalm 23 and elsewhere in the Bible is the supreme God who is in total control of the universe and all that happens in your life.

Look at the way Lord is written in Psalm 23:1 in your Bible.

Is it written like this—"LORD"? In this passage David uses a special word for Lord to refer to the Old Testament name that God gave Himself—YHWH (the Hebrew Scriptures had no vowels).

In the Hebrew Bible YHWH was probably pronounced Yahweh. *Jehovah* is the English translation of this name. So sacred was the name YHWH that Jewish high priests would only pronounce it once a year in the temple, and even then only behind the veil in the Holiest of Holies. It means "the self-existing One who has never had a beginning—One who will never have an end—the great I AM."

Did you notice that the title God chose to describe Himself is an incomplete sentence? Most people would finish that sentence—"I am love" or "I am light" or "I am . . ." But not our Lord. He purposefully did not complete the sentence. "I AM." He ever exists. He is always God. He is.

Are you hungry? He is the bread. Are you in the dark? He is the light. Are you searching? He is the truth. Are you lost? He is the way. Are you in need? He is the Shepherd.

Not only is He *the* Shepherd—He is *your* Shepherd. He is *my* Shepherd. Evangelist Angel Martinez has described our Shepherd in this way:

> The LORD, the One who made the world and everything that is in it, the One who lit the taper of the sun and put the stars in their places, that's my Shepherd. The One who threw a carpet of green grass upon the earth and tacked it down with

flowers, the One who scooped up the valleys and piled up the hills, the One who took the song of the seraph and robed it with feathers and gave it to the nightingale, the One who took the rainbow and wove it into a scarf and threw it about the shoulders of a dying storm, that's my Shepherd. At evening time, He pulls down the shade of the night and shoots it through with sunset fire. That's my Shepherd.

Indeed, that's our Shepherd. He is all that, and so much more.

David now declares who the Lord is—He "is my shepherd." Not, "He was my shepherd when I was young and inexperienced and needed someone to guide me." Not, "He will be my shepherd when I'm good enough to earn a relationship with Him." But, "He is my shepherd. Right now I can call him my shepherd."

When we say "Lord," we think of God's deity. When we say "my Shepherd," we think of God's humanity. God in human form—Jesus Christ—prophesied in the Old Testament and revealed in the New Testament. The Jehovah of the Old Testament is the Jesus of the New Testament.

Here is the wonderful news about salvation. In the Lord Jesus we meet the sovereign God—He is supremely in control. We also find sympathy—He understands our deepest needs. He is a king and a shepherd! He is the One who is a shepherd to millions and a shepherd to me!

The Lord Jesus is described as a shepherd three times in the

New Testament. He is the Good Shepherd, the Great Shepherd, and the Chief Shepherd.

The Good Shepherd

Jesus said, "I am the good shepherd; I know my sheep and my sheep know me—just as the Father knows me and I know the Father—and I lay down my life for the sheep" (John 10:14-15, NIV). Many shepherds may lose their lives for their sheep due to circumstances beyond their control. But that is not what Jesus is saying. He *chose* to lay down His life for the sheep.

To guard against predators, a shepherd will sleep at the door, or gate, of the sheepfold. His sheep mean everything to him. They are his livelihood. Even when he sleeps, it will be with one eye open, so he can be awakened at even the slightest hint of danger.

He chooses to lay down his life.

The true depth of the love of the Good Shepherd becomes apparent when you consider a very important truth—Jesus Christ is the only person who ever chose to die. But wait a minute, you may say, what about those kamikaze pilots in World War II? Or what about soldiers who, having heard the ominous click of a land mine, stood still until their buddies could scurry to safety? None of those men chose to die in the final sense of the word—they only chose *when* to die.

You and I, and everyone before us and yet to be born, will

die eventually. But only one person, the Good Shepherd, did not *have* to die. Hebrews 13:8 says, "Jesus Christ the same yesterday, and today, and for ever." Jesus is the God who was, and is, and is to come. He has always been, and He forever will be. Jesus did not *have* to die—He *chose* to die. If you and I were free from the condemnation of sin, would we choose to die so another could be saved?

Jesus said, "No man taketh [my life] from me, but I lay it down of myself" (John 10:18). Nails didn't hold our Savior to the tree. Silver cords of love and golden bonds of redemption held Him there. In the Good Shepherd's Kingdom, the Shepherd dies for the sheep.

The Great Shepherd

The Good Shepherd not only *died* for you—He *lives* for you! And that makes Him the Great Shepherd!

Now the God of peace, that brought again from the dead our Lord Jesus, that great shepherd of the sheep, through the blood of the everlasting covenant, make you perfect in every good work to do his will, working in you that which is well-pleasing in his sight, through Jesus Christ; to whom be glory for ever and ever. Amen.
—HEBREWS 13:20-21

The Good Shepherd was the One who willingly laid down His life for the sheep. Then, just as He said He would (John 10:18), He became the Great Shepherd—the risen King!

Surely, it was necessary for Him to die for our sins (Romans

5:12-19; 2 Corinthians 5:21). And it was just as necessary for Him to be raised from the dead. Paul wrote, "If Christ has not been raised, your faith is futile; you are still in your sins. . . . If only for this life we have hope in Christ, we are to be pitied more than all men" (1 Corinthians 15:17-18, NIV).

How does a flock benefit when their shepherd dies for them? Yes, he spent his precious life to save them, but the reality is, they are now left without him! They've lost their only source of protection. They're exposed and vulnerable to predators! They have no one to lead them to green pastures and still waters. The sheep would have a pitiful future if their story ended there.

But praise God—our story has a happy ending! Christ is risen! The Great Shepherd of the sheep is victoriously alive today. Hebrews says that He has been "brought again from the dead"! Also, Paul reminds us that Jesus is sitting at the right hand of God at this very moment, interceding on our behalf (Romans 8:34). And His prayers are always answered.

When the problems of your life are over your head, remember that they are under His feet. In 1 Corinthians 15:27 we are told, "For he [the Father] hath put all things under his [Jesus'] feet." Where is His head? It is in the heavenlies interceding for you. Where are your problems? Under His feet. The Great Shepherd is risen and waiting in the wings to return for you!

The Chief Shepherd

"And when the chief Shepherd shall appear, ye shall receive a crown of glory that fadeth not away" (1 Peter 5:4). Our Chief Shepherd will triumphantly return! I see the signs of His imminent return in the headlines of our world and in the heartaches of God's people. Indeed, His creation is groaning for His return.

I believe our Lord is at the door of heaven, getting ready for His glorious return. I believe that He is making ready the day when He will call His sheep homeward. I believe the skies are about to part, and the trumpet to sound, and we will see the Chief Shepherd appear! Hardly a day goes by that I don't yearn for that joyful day. I know you do too!

As the Good Shepherd, He dealt with the penalty of sin. As the Great Shepherd, He deals with the power of sin. As the Chief Shepherd, He's coming to take us away from the very presence of sin.

Every passage of Scripture has a key to its understanding, and in Psalm 23 David hung the key right on the front door! To trust as David trusted, we must know not only *whom* David knew, but also *what* David knew. He knew the sovereign God—Jehovah. He knew the Shepherd—Jesus—the secret of satisfaction.

People will disappoint us. Positions will be eliminated. Plans will be subverted. Possessions will be lost. Our only hope for genuine satisfaction is in a personal, permanent, protected relationship with Jesus Christ.

Do you know that God made you for Himself? Acts 17:28 says, "For in him we live, and move, and have our being." You'll never be satisfied apart from Him. It's not what He gives us that satisfies—it is Himself. Only when you begin a personal relationship with Jesus do you discover the secret of satisfaction.

> *Friends all around me are trying to find,*
> *What the heart yearns for by sin undermined.*
> *I have the secret, I know where 'tis found.*
> *Only true pleasures in Jesus abound.*
>
> *Jesus is all this world needs today.*
> *Blindly men strive, for sin darkens their way.*
> *Oh, to pull back the grim curtains of night.*
> *One look at Jesus and all will be light.*

If you've fussed and fumed through life's challenges, wondering if the Sovereign Creator of the universe was on vacation . . . if the Shepherd was napping under a shade tree during the most difficult times of your life . . . I have a message for you: The Lord is your Shepherd. The God who hung the stars. The God who poured the oceans. The God who raised the mountains. The God who knew you before you were knit together in your mother's womb. He is your Shepherd.

Perfect contentment, the kind that David discovered, only comes when a person puts his or her complete trust in the Shepherd. You will never have true satisfaction until you can say, "The Lord is my Shepherd" and mean it. Then, and only then, can you confidently say, "I shall not want."

When you say, "my Shepherd," the Shepherd says, "My sheep."

To know and be known by God is the purest, sweetest form of intimacy. One way to know God is to know His names. I invite you to meditate on seven names of God, paired below with verses from Psalm 23 and so experience a deeper, fuller understanding of the Jehovah God who intimately knows you.

JEHOVAH-RA'AH The Lord, my shepherd (Psalm 23:1)	*The LORD is my shepherd;*
JEHOVAH-JIREH The Lord, my provider (Genesis 22:14)	*I shall not want.*
JEHOVAH-SHALOM The Lord, our peace (Judges 6:24)	*He maketh me to lie down in green pastures: he leadeth me beside the still waters.*
JEHOVAH-RAPHA The Lord, my healer (Exodus 15:26)	*He restoreth my soul:*
JEHOVAH-TSIDKENU The Lord, our righteousness (Jeremiah 23:6)	*He leadeth me in the paths of righteousness for his name's sake.*

JEHOVAH-SHAMAH The Lord, ever-present (Ezekiel 48:35)	*Yea, though I walk through the valley of the shadow of death, I will fear no evil: for thou art with me; thy rod and thy staff they comfort me*
JEHOVAH-NISSI The Lord, our banner (Exodus 17:15)	*Thou preparest a table before me in the presence of mine enemies:*
JEHOVAH-RAPHA The Lord, my healer (Exodus 15:26)	*Thou anointest my head with oil; my cup runneth over.*
JEHOVAH-JIREH The Lord, my provider (Genesis 22:14)	*Surely goodness and mercy shall follow me all the days of my life: and I will dwell in the house of the LORD for ever.*

There is only one way to know that the Lord is your Shepherd, and that is to make sure that the Shepherd is your Lord. Jesus said, "My sheep hear my voice, and I know them, and they follow me; and I give unto them eternal life; and they shall never perish, neither shall any man pluck them out of my hand" (John 10:27-28).

Earthly shepherds will lose their sheep, but the Good Shepherd has never lost one. Our relationship with Jesus, our Shepherd, is permanent. Maybe you've never asked Jesus Christ to be your Shepherd, but you can do that today by asking Him to forgive you of all your sins and to be Lord of your life.

Or perhaps you've made the Shepherd the Lord of your life but have not allowed Him to shepherd your life through your darkest hours and most difficult days. You can do that today by asking His forgiveness and surrendering your needs to Him.

When you are plucked from the depths of sin, you are placed in the very hand of God! You can't climb into the hand of God but can only be placed there. Hallelujah! Our efforts didn't get us there—His grace placed us there. And His love will keep us there forever. He is able to "keep you from falling, and to present you faultless before the presence of his glory" (Jude 24).

Our relationship with our sovereign King, our Shepherd Lord, is personal. He loves us unconditionally and desires intimate fellowship with us. The relationship is permanent. We cannot lose the salvation that our Savior has bought with His blood. It is protected. So He certainly can and will take care of our deepest needs.

A little girl misquoted Psalm 23 by saying, "The LORD is my Shepherd. I've got all I want." That is the secret of satisfaction—Jehovah your Shepherd, my Shepherd. We shall not want. In him are the wellsprings of our hearts' desires. Your needs and my needs will never be met until they are met in Christ. *He is the secret of satisfaction.*

We serve a God who is able, a shepherd who is available. A God in the heavens and a shepherd in our hearts.

Savior, Like a Shepherd Lead Us

Savior, like a Shepherd lead us, Much we need Thy tender care;
In Thy pleasant pastures feed us, For our use Thy folds prepare.
Blessed Jesus, Blessed Jesus. Thou hast bought us, Thine we are;
Blessed Jesus, Blessed Jesus, Thou hast bought us, Thine we are.

We are Thine, do Thou befriend us, Be the guardian of our way;
Keep Thy flock from sin defend us, Seek us when we go astray.
Blessed Jesus, Blessed Jesus, Hear Thy children when they pray;
Blessed Jesus, Blessed Jesus, Hear Thy children when they pray.

Early let us seek Thy favor; Early let us do Thy will;
Blessed Lord and only Savior, With Thy love our bosoms fill.
Blessed Jesus, Blessed Jesus, Thou hast loved us, love us still;
Blessed Jesus, Blessed Jesus, Thou hast loved us, love us still.

CHAPTER TWO

THE PERFECT SHEPHERD

What a fellowship, what a joy divine,

Leaning on the everlasting arms;

What a blessedness, what a peace is mine,

Leaning on the everlasting arms.

What have I to dread, what have I to fear,

Leaning on the everlasting arms?

I have blessed peace with my Lord so near,

Leaning on the everlasting arms.

ELISHA A. HOFFMAN

he canopy of a midnight sky and sparkling stars veil the ceiling of the shepherd's bedroom. The hard, cold ground becomes his less-than-comfortable bed. His quarters are the same as his sheep—a circular corral of stones in which the sheep are protected during the night. The shepherd himself becomes the door as he lies down to sleep across the only opening in the stone wall. No intruder can come in, and no sheep can wander out, without waking him first. It may not be the perfect place to get a good night's rest, but it is the chosen place of a shepherd.

Through the night the shepherd drifts in and out of sleep at the door of the sheepfold—always keeping an ear and eye alert to the needs of his flock. He listens for the presence of predators. He watches the sky for threatening weather. His only thought, his only care, is the protection of and provision for his prized possessions.

The stars fade one by one in the predawn advent of the day. The sheep, awakened by the comforting call of their shepherd, meander toward the gate. The grass is wet with dew. The air is cool. Hushed and unhurried, the sheep graze for hours by still waters, always under the watchful eye of their shepherd.

Just before the peak of high noon, it is time for the sheep to rest and chew on their cud. The sun's hot rays compel the shepherd to find a shady spot for his sheep to lie down and digest their morning meal. This is a critical time for sheep.

This is the time when their wool grows thick and their bodies grow stronger. As they take their places in the cool shade, the shepherd walks among his flock, speaking softly to his sheep and tending to their needs. Every shepherd knows how important it is for sheep to have a quiet time.

What a marvelous picture of contentment and peace! This is certainly the antithesis of our lives in the twentieth-century. We are rushed, anxious, and stressed. We cannot imagine what it would feel like to lie down without a worry or a care. And yet that is exactly how God wants us to lie down. Turning stress into rest begins when we trust the Shepherd to lead us to such a spiritual oasis.

THE NATURE OF SHEEP

Why would David say, "He maketh me to lie down"? Wouldn't you think sheep would *want* to lie down in lush, green pastures? You'd think the sight of such a scene would cause a stampede, not a forced march.

The key to understanding this statement lies in knowing about the nature of sheep. They are dependent, dumb, defenseless, directionless, and easily distracted. And the Bible compares us to sheep! Imagine that!

Sheep are dependent. Not only do they need a shepherd to provide nourishing food, clean water, and safe pastures, but they depend on someone else to help them when they are "cast," a helpless state. David laments over his exiled separation from God in Psalms 42 and 43 by crying out, "Why art thou cast down, O my soul?" He remembers the sweet fellowship he once shared with God and calls out to Him for deliverance.

Philip Keller, author of the classic *A Shepherd Looks at Psalm 23*, tells us that sheep become "cast" when for whatever reason they slip and fall. They roll over on their backs and cannot right themselves without the shepherd's assistance. They lie on their backs, utterly defenseless, until rescued. If the shepherd gets distracted, or if the sheep is out of his sight, bloating will occur from trapped gases in the animal's four stomachs. The circulation is thus cut off, and death is inevitable. The sheep must be rescued from its own demise.

Sheep are dumb. Or maybe I should be kinder and say they are less than intelligent, since the Bible compares you and me to sheep. When was the last time you went to the circus and saw trained sheep? You see horses, elephants, lions, tigers, even pigs, but I venture to say that you will never see a sheep in the center ring!

The truth is, sheep are not among the most intelligent of the animal species. Not only do they not learn well, but they are also not very discerning. They see water, so they drink—with no thought of sniffing the surface for a hint of chemical poisoning or examining the depths for disease-producing parasites.

Sheep are defenseless. Easy marks, they are harassed and helpless without a shepherd. Lions bite. Tigers claw. Bears crush. Mules kick. Snakes strike. But sheep are defenseless.

Let Thy goodness, like a fetter,
Bind my wandering heart to Thee.
Prone to wander—Lord, I feel it—
Prone to leave the God I love;
Here's my heart—O take and seal it,
Seal it for Thy courts above.

Sheep are easily distracted. A breeze kicking up some leaves will so distract and frighten sheep that a stampede ensues. Remember the phrase, "The grass is always greener on the other side"? Greener pastures distract sheep too.

The most disturbing distractions for sheep are the parasites and insects that torment them. All types of flies and ticks cause great stress for sheep. They will run into trees to kill the pests that invade their nasal passages. Have you ever had poison ivy and thought you'd go insane by the itching? Double that. No, triple that. Now you know the torment these pests bring. The shepherd goes to considerable lengths to rid his sheep of these pests, but his labor pays off in the end.

ALL WE LIKE SHEEP

Having seen five characteristics of sheep—all with which we can identify—it is not difficult to see why we often find ourselves under stress. Think about it for a minute.

We make the same mistakes repeatedly. If you haven't read it recently, take a refresher tour through Romans 7 and let Paul's testimony sink into your heart anew. In short, the apostle says that what he wants to do, he finds himself not doing. And what he doesn't want to do, he finds himself doing. Indeed, if you've ever been honest about your own life, you know what Paul is talking about. Does sin and our inability at times to conquer it produce stress in our lives? Most assuredly.

We are vulnerable to spiritual attack. Do we have an enemy? The Bible says we do. His name is Satan. His sole purpose in life is to drive a wedge between the believer and God—to convince the believer that God, not Satan, is the enemy. He uses fear, worry, doubt, suspicion, false guilt, bondage, an unforgiving spirit, and all kinds of temptation to bring the believer down.

We are prone to wander. Think back over your life for the past year, or the past month, or even the past week. Have you given God less than top priority? Have you ignored divine appointments He has given you to share His love because you had "better things to do"? Have you unwisely filled your free time with things that grieve His heart? If you're like me, you have to answer yes at least to some degree. Like sheep, it's easy to take a few steps without looking up and soon discover that the Shepherd is nowhere in sight. And guess who wandered away?

We are dependent on Him. If you're like most people, you don't realize your dependency on God until you're burned out from stress, whether self-induced or caused by circumstances beyond your control. Why is that? Paul says we are "earthen vessels," and one positive result of that is that it quickly becomes evident that "the excellency of the power [is] . . . of God, and not of us" (2 Corinthians 4:7). He fittingly describes our dependency on God in the midst of stress: "We are troubled on every side, yet not distressed; we are perplexed, but not in despair; persecuted, but not forsaken; cast down [there's our sheep analogy again], but not destroyed; always bearing about in the body the dying of the Lord Jesus, that the life also of Jesus might be made manifest in our body" (2 Corinthians 4:8-10). We are totally dependent on God so that the love of His Son may be made known to the world. Without Him, we are stress magnets!

WE NEED A SHEPHERD

Throughout the Psalms we read that we are the sheep of God's pasture (Psalm 79:13; 80:1; 95:7; 100:3). Do you ever get sick and have to stay in bed for a few days? If you're like most people, you lay there and wonder about the 1,001 things you could be doing. But God is making you rest. There could be several reasons for your needing to rest.

God may want to show you that you're repeating a destructive pattern in your life. The Good Shepherd may take you off the path, give you insight, and then gently lead you to a better way. Isaiah said, "All we like sheep have gone astray; we have turned every one to his own way" (Isaiah 53:6).

Or maybe the deceiver himself, Satan, is walking along the fringes of your life, just waiting to pounce on you (1 Peter 5:8). The Shepherd sees the big picture and may be leading you away from the front line of Satan's attack so He can bring you to a place of green pastures and still waters where the supernatural battle is not waging and where you are not in such immediate danger.

Or perhaps you are directionless about a decision you need to make. With the hurried pace of your life, you may think you can't afford to take a couple of days, or even one, to contemplate your options and plan your future. Your Shepherd, knowing best, gently leads you to green pastures and still waters to give your mind a rest. Peace floods your soul, and you're able to think more clearly.

What about those times in your life when you worked yourself to the point of total exhaustion (this can even happen while doing ministry)? Maybe someone told you, "Oh, just tie a knot and hang on! There are just a few more things to do!" Behind your accommodating smile, you realized that you were working in your own power and strength instead of the power of God, but you couldn't quite say no. Sometimes God wants us to let go of the rope because it is keeping us tied to destructive habits. The Shepherd wants us to trust Him and follow Him to green pastures and still waters.

Every good shepherd knows how important it is to lead his sheep to places of rest because without his guidance, his sheep wouldn't choose to rest, and they probably wouldn't choose the greenest of pastures either. The Good Shepherd will make you lie down in green pastures, and He will lead you beside still waters if you trust Him with all your heart. There is security in the Shepherd. There is sufficiency in the Shepherd. There is serenity in the Shepherd.

We have security in the Shepherd. Who knows you better than the One who created you? Who could possibly care more for you than the One who died for you? Who can lead you more wisely and lovingly than the One who knows the end from the beginning?

You can have security of soul and life because the One who loves you is compassionate, caring, and courageous. Matthew 9:36 says, "But when he saw the multitudes, he was moved with compassion on them, because they fainted, and were scattered abroad, as sheep having no shepherd." Isaiah 40:11 says, "He shall feed his flock like a shepherd: he shall gather the lambs with his arm, and carry them in his bosom, and shall gently lead those that are with young." There is no greater picture of courage than the picture of a Savior who lays down His life for His sheep in John 10. He is willing to experience death in order to save His sheep from the wolf that attacks them. The hireling flees, but the Shepherd stays and conquers death.

He also *counts* His sheep, not wanting even one to be lost. Each evening as the shepherd herds his sheep into the sheepfold, he counts them one by one. If there are supposed to be

100 and he counts only ninety-nine, he will immediately search for the lost one. Second Peter 3:9 says, "The Lord is not slack concerning his promise, as some men count slackness; but is long-suffering to us-ward, not willing that any should perish, but that all should come to repentance." Our Shepherd knows His sheep (John 10:14). He even counts the hairs on our head (Matthew 10:30)!

We can rest in green pastures and beside still waters when we know the One who brings us this kind of eternal security.

We have sufficiency in the Shepherd. The first verse of Psalm 23 says, "The LORD is my Shepherd; I shall not want." Why do we get stressed even though Jesus is our Shepherd? Jesus says that we're not to worry about what we will eat or what we will wear. Jesus said these are not of primary importance. Instead, "Seek ye first the kingdom of God, and his righteousness; and all these things shall be added unto you" (Matthew 6:33).

Our Shepherd wants healthy, strong sheep. When we enter into the Shepherd's green pastures and lie down beside His still waters, we will have our fill of His righteousness and will be blessed. When we hunger, we need to consume His Word. When we thirst, we need to drink from His Spirit. Jesus said, "I am the bread of life: he that cometh to me shall never hunger; and he that believeth on me shall never thirst" (John 6:35).

The problem comes when we put the cart before the horse.

We look for happiness in what He can do for us or give to us, rather than rejoicing in who He is! His name is "I AM." He didn't say, "My name is I GIVE" or "My name is I DO." He created us to find happiness in Him, the I AM. "I am your happiness. I am your sufficiency."

Happiness is not something you find by looking for it. Happiness is something you discover and experience as you serve Jesus.

We have serenity in the Shepherd. Why does the shepherd make his sheep lie down in green pastures? Because his sheep get stressed out from their unwise decisions, their battle scars, and their wanderings. They wouldn't choose to lie down and rest; the shepherd has to *make* them. Sound familiar?

When the Shepherd of our lives makes us lie down, He brings us to a place of complete rest and solitary quietness. It is then we can hear His voice as He walks with us, calling our name, speaking words of healing and peace. God desires to share a quiet place with us. "In returning and rest shall ye be saved; in quietness and in confidence shall be your strength" (Isaiah 30:15). "Be still, and know that I am God" (Psalm 46:10).

Serenity is found in quiet times with your Shepherd. When the sheep lies down, it chews its cud. It brings back up what it has already consumed and gets nourishment from it again. I know that is not the most pleasant of pictures, but it is a good illustration of what we are to be doing when our Shepherd makes us lie down in green pastures. We grow most when we listen or read God's Word, then sit back and meditate on its truth.

You see, most of us are too busy or distracted to be still and meditate. Psalm 1 says, "Blessed is the man that walketh not in the counsel of the ungodly, nor standeth in the way of sinners, nor sitteth in the seat of the scornful. But his delight is in the law of the LORD; and in his law doth he meditate day and night" (verses 1-2). Walking, standing, and sitting with the ungodly are all physical activities. God is calling us to rest with Him.

We are all like sheep. We all need a shepherd. Only in Jesus, the Good Shepherd, will you find security. Only in Jesus, the Great Shepherd, will you find sufficiency. Only in Jesus, the Chief Shepherd, will you find serenity.

Jesus, I Am Resting, Resting

Jesus, I am resting, resting, In the joy of what Thou art;
I am finding our the greatness, Of Thy living heart.
Thou hast bid me gaze upon Thee, and Thy beauty fills my soul.
For by Thy transforming power, Thou hast made me whole.

Simply trusting Thee, Lord Jesus, I behold Thee as Thou art;
And Thy love, so pure, so changeless, Satisfies my heart.
Satisfies its deepest longings, Meets, supplies its every need,
And surrounds me with its blessings, Thine is love indeed.

Ever lift Thy face upon me, As I work and wait for Thee;
Resting 'neath Thy smile, Lord Jesus, Earth's dark shadows flee.
Brightness of my Father's glory, Sunshine of my Father's face,
Keep me ever trusting, resting, Fill me with Thy grace. Amen.

41

CHAPTER THREE

THE SHEPHERD
OF THE SECOND CHANCE

O to grace how great a debtor

Daily I'm constrained to be!

Let Thy goodness like a fetter,

Bind my wandering heart to Thee.

Prone to wander—Lord, I feel it—

Prone to leave the God I love;

Here's my heart—O take and seal it,

Seal it for Thy courts above.

ROBERT ROBINSON, "COME, THOU FOUNT"

*E*very day we are faced with choices. Indeed, because God has given us a free will, our spiritual journey proceeds choice by choice. The first choice in our journey is to choose or not to choose Jesus Christ as our Lord and Savior. At the moment we choose to repent of our sin and accept the sacrifice of Christ's death on the cross as payment for our sins, we become righteous before God. And He will never seek to renegotiate our decision.

Paul describes this beautiful reconciliation of a sinner to God in this way:

> *Therefore if any man be in Christ, he is a new creature; old things are passed away; behold, all things are become new. . . . God was in Christ, reconciling the world unto himself, not imputing their trespasses unto them. . . . For he hath made him to be sin for us, who knew no sin; that we might be made the righteousness of God in him.*
> —2 CORINTHIANS 5:17, 19, 21

Before coming to Christ, we are slaves to sin. We are not free not to choose. Even if we reject Christ, we have made a choice. Jesus said, "Whosoever committeth sin is the servant of sin" (John 8:34). But He adds that if we accept Him as our Lord and Savior, then we are free: "If the Son therefore shall make you free, ye shall be free indeed" (John 8:36).

After we make our choice, our choice chooses for us. There are consequences for our choices—always. What happens if we make a bad choice? Do we have the discernment at that point to recognize our bad choice? Or do we blindly keep going? Sometimes unpleasant consequences are our only wake-up call to our bad choices.

What is God's reaction to our bad choices? He is in control. Our choices have not taken Him by surprise. As the Good Shepherd, He can prevail over our bad choices and restore His wandering sheep!

THE RESTORING MINISTRY OF THE SHEPHERD

Have you ever experienced the restoration of the Shepherd after you've wandered from the fold? If you're like most children of God, you have. Isaiah 53:6 says, "All we like sheep have gone astray; we have turned every one to his own way." Though this speaks of people generally, sadly it is also true of believers. In both cases, when a sheep decides to go his own way, the Shepherd must take action.

It may not feel like the most pleasant of experiences when the Shepherd begins the ministry of restoration, but as the author of Hebrews wisely said, "Now no chastening for the present seemeth to be joyous, but grievous: nevertheless, afterward it yieldeth the peaceable fruit of righteousness unto them which are exercised thereby" (12:11).

There are three reasons why our Shepherd lovingly steps in to restore His sheep. His method depends on the reason they wandered off the path of righteousness in the first place:

Reason for Restoration	Method of Restoration
stubborn sheep	rod of correction
straying sheep	staff of guidance
sick sheep	oil of healing

The rod that restores the stubborn sheep. The shepherd's rod was a fascinating tool. The shepherd would dig up a sapling by hand in order to preserve the hard knob located just under the ground, a knob from which the roots descended. Then with his knife he would work at the knob until he had a round, smoothly finished ball. He would trim the sapling or rod to a few feet in length, then imbed pieces of metal into the knob. This was a club of protection with which to defend his sheep against robbers and wild animals, as well as a club of preservation with which to correct the ways of stubborn sheep.

Occasionally a sheep refuses to follow the shepherd's directions. Knowing his sheep may endanger itself, the shepherd has to step in and take drastic measures. Not out of malice, but out of love, the shepherd may even carefully break the leg of the stubborn sheep with his rod of correction. Immediately afterwards, the shepherd will bind the leg in a splint, carry the sheep on his shoulders, and pour oil on its leg to promote healing.

And then an amazing thing happens. When the bone heals and the splint is removed, the sheep that had been so stubborn is now the sheep that stays closest to the shepherd! A bond has been formed between sheep and shepherd that will never be broken. That once-stubborn sheep has become the most responsive sheep in the flock.

Is it possible that the Good Shepherd would resort to drastic measures—even pain—to correct the ways of a stubborn child of God? Hosea 6:1 says, "Come, and let us return unto the LORD: for he hath torn, and he will heal us; he hath smitten, and he will bind us up." And listen to the words of David: "Before I was afflicted I went astray: but now have I kept thy word" (Psalm 119:67).

"He hath smitten"—strong words, to be sure. But is that not exactly what God did when He used the rod of correction on the patriarch Jacob? After a brief allegiance to the Lord, Jacob proceeded to do things his own way. But as Jacob wandered, God watched. And one day God wrestled with Jacob as he was returning to Canaan—wounding him so much that he would never walk the same way again. His limp became a constant reminder of God's loving discipline.

Jacob became a wounded worshiper because God did not withhold the rod of correction. Someone has said, "If you are looking for a leader to follow, find someone with a limp." The wounded in life are those who have learned difficult lessons through suffering. Often their sight is clearer and their perception of God sharper because of the pain they have felt and the healing they have received.

Dear friend, we must not resist the Shepherd's rod of correction if it falls upon us. Is the wounding painful? Indeed. Does it seem that we will not be able to bear it? Most certainly. Then why would He subject us to such pain? Because the Shepherd is our Father who loves us so much that He is willing to hurt us to heal us. What we need to focus on is not our pain, but our Savior. God didn't save us just to take us to heaven. That's a fringe benefit. God saved us to make us holy as He is holy. The writer of Hebrews gives us God's perspective on His discipline:

My son, despise not thou the chastening of the Lord, nor faint when thou art rebuked of him; for whom the Lord loveth he chasteneth, and scourgeth every son whom he receiveth. . . . Now no chastening for the present seemeth to be joyous, but grievous: nevertheless, afterward it yieldeth the peaceable fruit of righteousness unto them which are exercised thereby.

—HEBREWS 12:5-6, 11

Receiving the Shepherd's correction will reveal our sonship to our Father, renew our worship of our Father, restore our fellowship with our Father, and reaffirm our reverence for our Father. Four good reasons to receive the rod.

The staff that restores the straying sheep. The staff is the most recognizable shepherd's tool. It is usually considered a gentle reminder of the shepherd's love for his flock. With his staff the shepherd restores straying sheep back to the fold and guides his flock along steep, rocky trails. The shepherd also uses his staff to push away branches while leading his sheep through narrow, thorny passages.

To make a staff, the shepherd cuts the sapling above ground. Though it is green and pliable, he will soak the sapling in water to soften it even more. Then he will bend the top of the staff over to form a crook and will tie it in position until it is dry and seasoned. The hook is just the right size for reaching around the chest of a lamb or around the neck of a larger sheep.

Carelessness, not defiance, is usually the reason sheep stray from the fold. They simply do what all sheep do—nibble a little here, nibble a little there, poke around here, poke around there. Pretty soon they've nibbled their way right out of the pasture and maybe into trouble.

They may slip over a steep ravine, entangle themselves in a thornbush, or stumble into a rocky creek bed. Maybe they're running from the heated pursuit of a mountain lion! What the shepherd needs for a straying sheep is not the rod of correction but the staff of guidance.

Surely the staff was the instrument David was thinking about when he wrote, "I waited patiently for the LORD; and he inclined unto me, and heard my cry. He brought me up also out of a horrible pit, out of the miry clay, and set my feet upon a rock, and established my goings" (Psalm 40:1-2).

The oil that restores the sick sheep. At night, when the shepherd would lead the sheep back into the sheepfold, not only did he count the sheep, but he called them each by name. He moved among them, caressing their coats while looking for hints of disease or wounds. A mixture of oil, sulfur, and tar was applied, not only as a healing agent to comfort his suffering sheep, but also as an insecticide to keep flies out of a wound and to promote healing.

Isn't this a beautiful picture of the Shepherd's tender love? He leads us home. He comes alongside us, calling us by name. He touches us. And before we can point to our broken places and wounded hearts, He is already rubbing the balm of His Spirit's healing into our lives.

How often we go through life, presenting to the outside world a thick-skinned, "I can do it all" image. But all along the way our Shepherd knows thoroughly our deepest needs. It is the ministry of the Shepherd that restores us when we fail, picks us up when we fall, and strengthens us when we are weak. He is the One who ministers to us all, a needy flock indeed.

"Thou lovest righteousness, and hatest wickedness: therefore God, thy God, hath anointed thee with the oil of gladness above thy fellows," says David in Psalm 45:7. Thank God for His ministry of chastisement, correction, and comfort!

But once we are restored to the path of righteousness, how do we stay there? How can we keep from having to be constantly corrected, directed, and protected? By submitting to the mastery of the Shepherd.

THE RIGHTEOUS MASTERY
OF THE SHEPHERD

Once the Shepherd has restored us from our wayward journey, He leads us onto the path of righteousness. A pathway that is level at the foot of the cross of our crucified Lord and before the throne of our risen King. A pathway of light that illumines our way to Him. A pathway of liberation that frees us from our slavery to sin and gives us the freedom to choose the way of Calvary.

Many believers have the mistaken idea that it is acceptable to live in a constant state of restoration. Of course, God compassionately restores everyone in His flock whenever there is a need. But the believer must realize that life is meant to be lived on the path, not in the past.

How can we stay on the path, close to the Shepherd? How many times must we fall and slip before we learn to stay close to the Shepherd? We ought to be like the sheep with the broken leg that nuzzles closer to the shepherd as a result of its brokenness.

Perhaps what we need most is to hear His voice. Listen to Jesus' words about why the sheep stay close to Him:

To [the shepherd of the sheep] the porter openeth; and the sheep hear his voice: and he calleth his own sheep by name, and leadeth them out. And when he putteth forth his own sheep, he goeth before them, and the sheep follow him: for they know his voice. And a stranger will they not follow, but will flee from him; for they know not the voice of strangers.

—JOHN 10:3-5

How do we submit to the mastery of the Shepherd?

Listen to the Shepherd. "The sheep hear his voice." His voice must be the first we listen for and the first we obey. You can't obey a voice you don't hear. Further, where He is going, we must follow. Our eyes, our ears, our entire focus must be on Him. We need to spend time in the green pastures, meditating upon the Word of God.

Four times in the Bible we are commanded to "hear his voice" and "harden not your hearts" (Psalm 95:7-8; Hebrews 3:7-8; 3:15; 4:7). Why are we exhorted not to harden our hearts? From what we've learned about sheep, we know that we're stubborn creatures who are prone to resist anyone or anything that prevents us from getting our own way.

When our Lord wanted us to listen, He would say, "He who has ears to hear, let him hear." His voice is a mandate for action. And the only way we will be sure it is His voice we are hearing is to hear it so often, so consistently, and so appreciatively that a stranger's voice—the voice of the world, the flesh, or the devil—is instantly recognized and refused.

The United States government doesn't use fake money to teach Treasury agents to detect counterfeit bills. They show them real dollars over and over and over until they have every little detail memorized. When a counterfeit is put in front of them, they recognize it instantly because it doesn't fit the pattern their eyes are looking for. It is far wiser to spend time learning the one true voice than it is trying to learn to detect a multitude of false voices.

Look to the Shepherd. Because sheep have poor eyesight, the only way they can see where the shepherd is leading is to stay close to him. The application is clear—"Don't wander off!" This involves more than watching—it entails staying close to the Lord and hanging on His every word.

Love the Shepherd. Have you ever adored someone? You wanted to be with him or her all the time. You wanted to show him or her your love. It's the same with us and Jesus. To respond to the mastery of the Shepherd is to act in obedience to His calling of godliness in our lives. Jesus said, "If ye keep my commandments, ye shall abide in my love; even as I have kept my Father's commandments, and abide in his love" (John 15:10).

The story of Mary and Martha in Luke 10 offers a clear picture of how we are to listen to, look to, and love our Shepherd. Martha was busily doing her household duties, and Mary sat at the feet of Jesus. When Martha complained to Jesus about Mary's lack of help, Jesus responded, "Martha, Martha, thou art careful and troubled about many things: but one thing is needful; and Mary hath chosen that good part, which shall not be taken away from her" (Luke 10:41-42). Mary chose to sit at the feet of her Shepherd, listening to His every word, looking to the One who had rescued her, loving the One who had restored her to righteousness.

Mary had wandered, was restored to the fold, and now was like the sheep that remained most loyal to the Shepherd after being broken. That's the way we should be when we are restored. This is more than an obligation—it's spiritual devotion!

If I had to identify the major misconception held by believers today when they think of the mastery of their Shepherd, it would be that they spend too much time asking the Master to get them out of trouble instead of asking Him to mature them in righteousness! We too often live on the defensive instead of the offensive.

A standout college football player, upon graduation, was asked by his coach to help recruit high school seniors. The star graduate was more than willing to do so.

"Now, John, let me tell you the kind of recruit we're looking for."

"Right, coach."

"You know the guy who stays down when he gets knocked down? That's not the guy we want."

"Right, coach."

"You know the guy who gets knocked down but gets back

up and gets knocked down again and then stays down? That's not the guy we want either."

"Right, coach."

"You know the guy who gets knocked down and gets up time after time? The one who gets up every time he gets knocked down?"

"That's the guy we want, right, coach?"

"No, that's not the guy either. I want you to find the guy who's knocking everybody down. That's the guy we want!"

We need to move beyond the defensive line of Christianity and go on the offensive—advancing the Kingdom, fulfilling the Great Commission, telling others about Jesus. Our Shepherd will never lead us where His strength cannot keep us. He will never lead us down a path that He hasn't first walked down Himself. "The people that do know their God shall be strong, and do exploits" (Daniel 11:32).

THE REGAL MAJESTY
OF THE SHEPHERD

He leads us "for his name's sake." Don't be mistaken—this is not an egotistical effort by the Shepherd to make His name look good. It goes much deeper than that. God's honor is at stake by the way you and I live.

You will recall that the name David uses when he talks about the Lord in Psalm 23:1 is YHWH (Yahweh), meaning "I AM THAT I AM." If the followers of the Holy One of Israel are not walking in righteous paths, what will people say about the One who is leading them?

What would you think of a shepherd who had a flock of sheep that were gaunt from undernourishment, scarred from injuries, restless from nagging pests, and roaming aimlessly on a hillside? What if the pasture was teeming with poisonous weeds, insects, and filthy pools of stagnant water? If you were a sheep, would you trust a shepherd who spent most of his day napping in the shade, who didn't know a thing about animal husbandry, who didn't even own a rod and staff? You wouldn't. And neither would I. We would see the writing on the wall: "Enter at your own risk."

With our many limitations and weaknesses, we need a vigilant, compassionate, skillful shepherd to watch over us, lead us, guide us, and keep us on the path of righteousness. The condition of the flock speaks volumes about the character of the shepherd.

Yet, God doesn't need us to make Him look good. Our Shepherd is infinitely good. That fact is certain and unchanging. Regardless of how we live, He is Sovereign King, the Creator and Sustainer of all life!

Yet to a watching world, we can give the impression, by our choices, that He is not a good Shepherd. As people observe us, what are they seeing? If we rebel stubbornly against the

Shepherd and feel the rod of His correction, then complain or give the appearance that He is unfair, what will unbelievers think of our God? In reality, we are the problem, not Him. If we respond in unfairness, then we are in essence saying, "Our God is not a good Shepherd."

When He restores us and leads us onto the path of right-eousness, it is not only for our benefit and His glory but for those who do not know the Good Shepherd—those who have been wandering the hillsides and are injured, undernour-ished, wounded. They're looking for a Good Shepherd like ours, a Shepherd who is strong, gentle, compassionate, and courageous. They're looking for a Shepherd who will take them into His fold and give them the protection they need.

When we walk in "paths of righteous-ness for his name's sake," it is so that those sheep who have not heard His name can see that the great I AM is the owner and guardian of the flock. We are walking on the pathway of righteousness so that His glory may be known to a watch-ing world. There ought to be a burn-ing desire in our hearts to give glory to His name.

We are reflections of Him not only to others we see in church on Sunday, but also to our neighbors, to the grocery store clerk, to our child's schoolteacher, to our coworkers. We

—◡

are to reflect the Good Shepherd to a lost and dying world. Second Corinthians 2:15-16 (NIV) says, "For we are to God the aroma of Christ among those who are being saved and those who are perishing. To the one we are the smell of death; to the other, we are the fragrance of life."

What kind of picture are you and I giving to those who look at the flock of God? What do they think of our Shepherd as a result of the condition of our lives? We are the sheep of His pasture, and to encourage other needy sheep to join His flock, we must show that He satisfies our deepest longings, gives us rest, picks us up when we fall, and keeps us standing.

All the Way My Savior Leads Me

All the way my Savior leads me—What have I to ask beside?
Can I doubt His tender mercy, Who through life has been my guide?
Heavenly peace, divinest comfort, Here by faith in Him to dwell!
For I know, whate'er befall me, Jesus doeth all things well;
For I know, whate'er befall me, Jesus doeth all things well.

All the way my Savior leads me—Cheers each winding path I tread,
Gives me grace for every trial, Feeds me with the living bread.
Though my weary steps may falter, And my soul a-thirst may be,
Gushing from the Rock before me, Lo! a spring of joy I see;
Gushing from the Rock before me, Lo! a spring of joy I see.

All the way my Savior leads me—O the fullness of His love!
Perfect rest to me is promised, In my Father's house above.
When my spirit, clothed immortal, Wings its flight to realms of day,
This my song through endless ages: Jesus led me all the way;
This my song through endless ages: Jesus led me all the way.

CHAPTER FOUR

THE SHEPHERD OF THE DYING

Sometimes on the mount where the sun shines so bright,

God leads His dear children along;

Sometimes in the valley, in darkest of night,

God leads His dear children along.

Some thru the waters, some thru the flood,

Some thru the fire, but all thru the blood;

Some thru great sorrow, but God gives a song,

In the night season and all the day long.

G. A. YOUNG

A certain woman walked with God for many, many years. She was a saint by every measure of the word. At last her body grew frail, and her life began to ebb away. Near the end, her loved ones gathered around her, weeping and wringing their hands in grief. As she looked at them, instead of joining in their mourning, she said, "Go ahead and cry if you must; but don't cry for me. I'm tickled to death to die." I like that. Tickled to death to die.

When was the last time you had a cheerful discussion with someone about death? Just mentioning the word causes many people to change the topic as quickly as they change the channel on their television. Now, I don't mean to make light of the subject, because I have experienced deep grief and have wondered how I will face my own death and the death of my wife and family. I simply want us to learn to embrace death as a friend instead of a foe.

Man is the only creature who knows he is going to die and tries desperately to forget it! What causes this fear of death? I think we all tend to fear the unknown. And perhaps we are not totally confident that what the Bible says about life after death is true. Perhaps we fear the pain or suffering that we may have to endure before we die. We may wonder if we will have the courage to face those final hours of life without falling apart. Many of us we spend much time and money trying to obscure the fact that we're winding down to the grave. But actually, if we know Christ, death is something we ought to anticipate with confidence and even joy.

Charles Haddon Spurgeon said about death, "Death has no power to suspend the music of a Christian's heart, but rather makes that music become more sweet, more clear, more heavenly, till the last kind act which death can do is to let the earthly strain melt into the heavenly chorus, the temporal joy into the eternal bliss! Let us have confidence, then, in the blessed Spirit's power to comfort us. . . . You know not what joys may be stored up for you in the cottage around which grace will plant the roses of content."

"Eternal bliss." That's how Spurgeon described death. Surely, this should be our response as well.

Before we begin to draw analogies as to what this "valley" in Psalm 23 could mean, I'd like to mention a valley in Palestine actually called "the valley of the shadow of death." It originated centuries ago beside a freshwater stream in a valley located between Bethlehem and Jerusalem (about 2,700 feet above sea level) and travels down to the Dead Sea, 1,300 feet below sea level.

The stream, fed by overflowing torrents from the surrounding hillsides during the rainy season, created a craggy valley that was deep and narrow—sometimes only about twelve inches wide! This dark, foreboding place was full of shadows and dark turns, even at high noon. Dangerous predators would hide in the cracks in the rock, ready to pounce on an unsuspecting sheep or shepherd. Robbers also claimed this valley as a favorite hideout.

Yet despite its drawbacks, this valley was very useful. It provided a natural trail for shepherds to get their flocks from the highlands near Bethlehem to the lowlands at Jericho. In the wintertime when there was a scarcity of grass, shepherds would lead their sheep through the valley to Jericho where the grass was green even in the wintertime. When spring would come, the shepherds would lead their sheep through the valley to green pastures in the highlands.

No doubt David led his sheep through this "valley of the shadow of death." It was probably during these times as a young shepherd boy that he learned to trust in a great Jehovah who would protect him and his sheep through great travails. Even though he never knew what danger might lurk around the next turn, he did not allow his fears to overshadow his faith. God was his protector. David, like his Shepherd, learned to smile at death.

D E A T H   A   D E C I D E D   F A C T

The first principle that will help strengthen your confidence in the future and help remove your fear of death is that death is an indisputable reality. Last time I checked, this statistic still held true: one out of one dies.

Hebrews 9:27 says, ". . . it is appointed unto men once to die, but after this the judgment." Death is certain for all of us. We each have an appointment with our Lord. The only excep-

tion is if Jesus comes first. We are born—we live—we die—
we stand before the judgment-seat of Christ.

Romans 5:12 explains that we all die because of sin, which
is also the reason for judgment. Sin entered the world through
Adam and Eve and brought death with it, physically and spiritually. Then as sin spread to all men as part of the constitu-
tion of the human race, death spread right along with it.
Wherever sin goes, death follows. Death is a stubborn fact.

Since neither you nor I know the hour of our death or the
moment of His return, we should count on what we do know—
death is a certain fact, one for which we dare not *not* prepare.

The time of our death is the perplexing mystery. It
is one thing to accept as certain the fact that we
will all die; it is another thing to accept the
uncertainty of its timing. I've heard someone say
that we live our lives a heartbeat away from
eternity.

The writer of Proverbs knew this: "Boast not
thyself of tomorrow; for thou knowest not what
a day may bring forth" (Proverbs 27:1). James, our
Lord's half-brother, expounded on this further:

*Go to now, ye that say, Today or tomorrow we will go into such a city,
and continue there a year, and buy and sell, and get gain: whereas ye
know not what shall be on the morrow. For what is your life? It is even
a vapor, that appeareth for a little time, and then vanisheth away.*
—JAMES 4:13-14

Taken by themselves, you could interpret these verses to be fatalistic—as if life were a game of chance. Yet, these verses are not a commentary on the plan of God; they are primarily a warning against the arrogance of man.

When you hear the early-morning radio weatherman say there's a 100 percent chance of rain, what is your response? You prepare—coat, umbrella, extra driving time. You are certain that it's going to rain. You don't know exactly when, but you know it will be today. You're not arrogant about it, but you are prepared. We should respond in a similar way to death.

Our lives are like a vapor of breath on a frosty morning— here for a moment, then gone. Our confidence comes from knowing who gives that breath and who will stop giving that breath at the moment He chooses. God doesn't take our lives—He simply stops giving us life.

Death is a personal matter. This message is for you. This message is for me. We are living on the very precipice of eternity. Just over the other side is our future— one that will be spent either in heaven with our Lord or in the lake of fire with the enemy of our souls. Where will you be forever?

If you knew you were going to die tomorrow, what would you do differently today? Apologize to your spouse and your family for losing your temper last night? Go to an estranged friend you haven't seen in a while and make amends? Check on your finances to make sure your family will be taken care of when you're gone? Share the Gospel with a neighbor you've been avoiding?

When David says, "*I walk through the valley of the shadow of death,*" he's talking about himself. You and I are in the shadow of death every day. Whether we know it or not, like it or not, accept it or not, death is a personal matter we dare not ignore. My friend, you may die at any moment, no matter how healthy you may feel. And since you do not have the keys to the kingdom on the other side, you don't know when the door is going to be opened for you to go through it. To be forewarned should be to be forearmed.

DEATH A DEFEATED FOE

Yes, we are all going to walk through "the valley of the shadow of death," but if we know Christ, we do not need to be afraid because our Shepherd is with us. Jesus has defeated this foe. He has given us the victory over death. First Corinthians 15:55-57 says, "O death, where is thy sting? O grave, where is thy victory? The sting of death is sin; and the strength of sin is the law. But thanks be to God, which giveth us the victory through our Lord Jesus Christ."

There are no valleys without mountains. It is geographically impossible to have a valley without a mountain. They are beautiful complements in God's grand creation. If you find yourself in a valley, you have necessarily come down from a mountain. If you're on a mountain, you came to that place by way of a valley.

Psalm 23 is a valley Psalm between two glorious mountain peaks. In Psalm 22 we climb the blood-drenched slopes of Mount Calvary, where the Good Shepherd laid down His life for His sheep. On the other side of the valley are the sunlit peaks of Mount Zion in Psalm 24—a picture of the Chief Shepherd who will someday return for His sheep.

Just as David traveled through the valley armed with his rod and staff to protect his sheep, the Good Shepherd of Psalm 23 leads, protects, and comforts us through whatever trials may befall us. He is equipped with whatever we need to be victorious. Like David, when we turn to Him in absolute trust, we will fear no evil.

There is no shadow without light. Imagine being in a cave without a flashlight. Can you see any shadows? No. You cannot even see your hand! Shadows are only visible in the presence of light. Regardless of how dark, how large, how absolutely ominous a shadow appears, it is only there because light is also there.

The wife of a great preacher died when she was still a very young woman. They had a young daughter who didn't understand all of the intricacies surrounding her mother's death and how Jesus' death provided eternal life for her mother. A few days after the funeral, the father and daughter were driving downtown. The girl looked at the wall of a department store and saw a large shadow of a small truck. She said, "Daddy, look at that big shadow." Right then and there, the father thought of a great lesson to teach his daughter. He said, "Sweetheart, if you had a choice, would you rather be hit by the shadow of the truck or by the truck?" She said, "That's easy, Daddy, the shadow." He responded, "Honey, it was only the shadow that hit Mama. The truck hit Jesus 2,000 years ago at Calvary."

Jesus has taken the sting out of sin and the fear out of the grave. He has become our victor. Through the Holy Spirit He has given us the assurance that He will always be with us and will always watch over us. Isaiah 9:2 says, "The people that walked in darkness have seen a great light: they that dwell in the land of the shadow of death, upon them hath the light shined."

". . . through the tender mercy of our God; whereby the dayspring from on high hath visited us, to give light to them that sit in darkness and in the shadow of death, to guide our feet into the way of peace."
—LUKE 1:78-79

There is no evil without a greater good. Are you facing a fearful shadow, perhaps even the shadow of death? There can be no such shadow without there being a greater light.

The One who created the valley is there with you! He has prepared the way *through* the valley. It is not a place of permanence, but of passage. The Shepherd knows every twist and turn, every changing shadow, every den where danger lurks—and He is with you always and forever!

We need to focus on the light and not the darkness. I know that sounds easy, but how often have you asked for deliverance from something instead of asking God to show you more of Himself through the trial? As Don Baker, a well-known author and speaker, said, "We would all like to be air-lifted to spiritual gianthood." But God wants us to walk through the shadows.

"Ye are of God, little children, and have overcome them: because greater is he that is in you, than he that is in the world" (1 John 4:4). When the shadow approaches and you have to walk through it, fear no evil, for He is with you! The One who is greater than death is in you! He is your Jehovah-shamah—the Lord ever-present (Ezekiel 48:35). Whatever your trial, His grace is greater, His peace is purer, His devotion is dearer. Wherever Satan casts a shadow, our sovereign Lord still reigns supreme, and we can walk in His light.

DEATH A DEVOTED FRIEND

I can just imagine what you're thinking. *Death is a friend?* Yes, it is, if you know Jesus Christ. I spent considerable time debating this expression, realizing that the word *friend* depicts an emotional bond between two people. A friend is someone who helps you, someone you trust, someone who is on your side. Can we trust death? Can death help us? If we remember that for the child of God death is simply the entrance into eternal bliss with God, then yes, death can be our friend.

Death is not an arbitrary, uncontrolled power roaming

throughout the world. Death is an instrument that is placed solely in the hands of our sovereign, loving Lord. The psalmist says, "Precious in the sight of the LORD is the death of his saints" (Psalm 116:15). Here *precious* does not mean emotionally or highly valued so much as carefully attended or watched over by God. Children of God do not die randomly, accidentally, or unobserved. Rather, they die in His sight, in His time, for His benevolent purpose.

Death is for our benefit. *Physically*, those who die in Christ gain freedom from pain and temptation. *Mentally*, those who die in Christ gain liberation of mind and perfect heavenly wisdom. *Socially*, those who die in Christ gain friends and experience an eternal reunion with loved ones. *Spiritually*, those who die in Christ gain the pure, undefiled, uninterrupted enjoyment of the presence of God. We will be made like Christ in the next life.

As David led his flocks through dark valleys, do you think he ever wondered if he and his flock would arrive safely? No doubt he had such thoughts, but they were fleeting. They crossed his mind but didn't stay. He was going *through* the valley. Instead, he meditated on three truths that allowed him to "fear no evil"—the purpose, presence, and power of the Shepherd.

The purpose of the Shepherd. "Yea, though I walk through the valley of the shadow of death, I will fear no evil." The Shepherd leads us *through* the valley. This is a journey that goes somewhere. The valley is not a box canyon. Jesus has kicked the end out of the grave. The shepherd would never lead his sheep through a barren place unless he was going to a better place.

First Chronicles 29:15 says, "For we are strangers before thee, and sojourners, as were all our fathers: our days on the earth are as a shadow, and there is none abiding." We are here for a season, and when that time is through and His purposes for our lives are accomplished, we will go home to live with Him forever.

The presence of the Shepherd. ". . . for thou art with me." Up until verse 4, David spoke *of* the Lord. Now he is speaking *to* the Lord, as if he is sitting in His presence before the throne.

Nothing will bring you face-to-face with God more than going through the dark valleys of life. When you are there, you will cling to His garments and hold on to His hand. You won't stray far from the fold when you're in the dark.

Jesus said, "I will not leave you as orphans, I will come to you" (John 14:18, NIV). The Shepherd is ever-present with us through the presence of His Spirit. Hebrews 13:5 says, ". . . for he hath said, I will never leave thee, nor forsake thee." Do you have that assurance today? Do you believe that He is with you? Isaiah 41:10 says, "Fear thou not; for I am with thee: be not dismayed; for I am thy God: I will strengthen thee; yea, I will help thee; yea, I will uphold thee with the right hand of my righteousness."

The ultimate Sovereign is our intimate Shepherd. You will not have to cross Jordan alone. You will not appear before the judgment of the Holy God alone. You are not going to die alone. "For thou art with me."

The power of the Shepherd. ". . . thy rod and thy staff they comfort me," David affirms. As you may recall from a previous chapter, the shepherd not only uses his rod to correct stubborn sheep, but also to protect his sheep. And the staff is used to lift and restore his sheep. There is power in both the rod and the staff of the Good Shepherd.

When you pass through "the valley of the shadow of death," His power will be there with you to sustain you. His rod will protect you from the powers of evil, and his staff will draw you close to Him. As your feet touch the chilly waters of the river of death, you'll be singing all the way. Romans 8:38-39 says, "For I am persuaded, that neither death . . . nor any creature, shall be able to separate us from the love of God, which is in Christ Jesus our Lord."

Whatever trial or difficulty you are going through, take comfort in knowing that it will pass. Our peace is forged in the fire of trials. Our trust rises from the ashes of hopelessness. Look at David's life. His humble beginnings laid the foundation upon which he built his unshakable faith in Jehovah-Jireh, his sovereign provider. Once he found such a Shepherd, he never stopped singing about Him.

A beautiful Puritan prayer from a book entitled *The Valley of Vision* sums up our journey of trust in our Shepherd:

Let me learn by paradox
that the way down is the way up,
that to be low is to be high,
that the broken heart is the healed heart,
that the contrite spirit is the rejoicing spirit,
that the repenting soul is the victorious soul,
that to have nothing is to possess all,
that to bear the cross is to wear the crown,
that to give is to receive,
that the valley is the place of vision.

Lord, in the daytime stars can be seen from deepest wells,
and the deeper the wells the brighter the stars shine;
Let me find thy light in my darkness,
thy life in my death,
thy joy in my sorrow,
thy grace in my sin,
thy riches in my poverty,
thy glory in my valley.

In Heavenly Love Abiding

In heavenly love abiding, No change my heart shall fear;
And safe is such confiding, For nothing changes here.
The storm may roar without me, My heart may low be laid.
But God is round about me, And can I be dismayed?

Wherever He may guide me, No fear shall turn me back;
My Shepherd is beside me, And nothing shall I lack.
His wisdom ever waketh, His sight is never dim;
He knows the way He taketh, And I will walk with Him.

Green pastures are before me, Which yet I have not seen;
Bright skies will son be o'er, Where darkest clouds have been.
My hope I cannot measure, My path to life is free;
My Savior is my treasure, And He will walk with me.

CHAPTER FIVE

THE SHEPHERD OF PLENTY

His love has no limit,

His grace has no measure,

His pow'r has no boundary known unto men;

For out of His infinite riches in Jesus,

He giveth and giveth and giveth again!

ANNIE JOHNSON FLINT
"HE GIVETH MORE GRACE"

*T*he devil wants you to live your life with an empty cup. He wants you to think that God's cup of grace has dried up for you. He wants you to be disenchanted with God. Most especially, he wants you to feel that God is a cosmic killjoy— that He is always thinking of ways to rob you of happiness and peace.

If you are a child of God and have begun to think this way, then Satan is really working on you! Our enemy knows that if you start to feel negatively about God, he can have his way with you in other areas of your life too.

Now remember, Satan is not omnipresent (everywhere at once), nor is he omniscient (all-knowing) or omnipotent (all-powerful). He has limited powers. He cannot thwart God's plans or change God's mind. He cannot reverse the destiny of his own fiery defeat (Revelation 20:10). But in spite of his limitations, Satan has ways of spreading lies about God among and within those who follow and trust Him.

Jesus said that Satan is "the father of lies" (John 8:44). This "father" title is perhaps due to his telling the first lie ever heard on earth. As soon as God had given instructions to Adam and Eve in the Garden of Eden, Satan came on the scene to corrupt the truth (Genesis 2:15—3:6). Prior to Satan's entrance into the Garden of Eden, nothing but truth had been heard on earth.

His very first words to Eve were an attempt to confuse her about what God had said—to make God look selfish, controlling, and restrictive. Next he attempted to deceive her by lying about God—an attempt to make God look powerless and paranoid. He told Eve that she and Adam would not die if they disobeyed God, that God had kept them away from the tree of knowledge of good and evil because He didn't want to share His power with them. To our eternal dismay, this second attack worked.

Now, before we judge our ancestors too quickly, let's ask ourselves how frequently we listen to the author of confusion and deception ourselves. Do we truly see God as One who gives sacrificially, who loves unconditionally, who shows mercy continually? Whether we do or not, He does love us like that, and we can trust Him always. He wants to give us victory!

The Good Shepherd goes with us through the valley leading us to tablelands of plenty in the presence of our enemies. And not only that, He honors and heals us with His oil of gladness, causing our cup to overflow!

OUR SHEPHERD FILLS OUR SOULS

Who sets the table at your house? For most of us, it depends on who is coming. When we have honored guests coming to our home for a special occasion, we give a lot of attention to setting the table. I say "we" liberally, because it is actually my wife who is the expert at hospitality. I usually retreat in a hurry, not because I'm unwilling to help, but because I'm not the one gifted with a sense of grace and beauty. Sometimes I cannot tell the difference between a salad plate and a bread plate, or a soup spoon from a teaspoon (or perhaps I don't want to know)!

Who prepares the table to which David comes? An archangel? Cherubim or seraphim? No. The table is prepared by the Lord Himself! The Lord of glory has prepared a table for us. He loves you. He loves me. And He welcomes us to be His honored guests at His table!

Just as shepherds must go before their sheep to prepare the grassy tableland, our Good Shepherd goes before us to prepare a table spread with good things to satisfy us and protect us from our enemies. Isaiah 41:17-20 is a beautiful description of the type of tableland the Good Shepherd prepares for His sheep:

When the poor and needy seek water, and there is none, and their tongue faileth for thirst, I the LORD will hear them, I the God of Israel will not forsake them. I will open rivers in high places, and fountains in the midst of the valleys: I will make the wilderness a pool of water, and the dry land springs of water . . . that they may see, and know, and consider, and understand together, that the hand of the LORD hath done this, and the Holy One of Israel hath created it.

Why is it important that this table is prepared "in the presence of mine enemies"?

In David's day it was customary to make treaties or

covenants among nations that were the enemies of Israel and of God. Usually a meal would follow this covenant agreement. David, as the shepherd-king of Israel, might be surrounded on all sides by these powerful kings. In the world's eyes, these kings were probably more powerful in manpower and resources than David's army. But in the eyes of heaven, none were mightier than David and his covenant partner, Jehovah!

Is Satan whispering that God is not with you in your daily battles? Is he whispering lies that God is going to erase your name from the book of life for something you've done but of which you have repented? Satan never had it so wrong! And David never had it so right! Salvation in Christ is not a funeral but a feast!

When in covenant with Jehovah, it doesn't matter how many or how fierce the enemies are—you have the victory! Are you a child of God? Then you share in an invincible covenant with Jehovah. You can say with David, "I will fear no evil: for thou art with me."

When Jesus Christ invited His disciples to drink from His cup in the upper room, you and I became partners with Him (compare Hebrews 13:20-21). His blood was shed to purchase our redemption and to restore us to covenant relationship with God. We sit at His table, in the presence of our enemies, with no fear. Why? Because when Satan attacks us, he is attacking the Lord Jesus Christ Himself. Our Great Shepherd fights our battles and has won the ultimate victory! Such is the protection, the provision, and the power of the covenant!

The Bible is a continual feast from Genesis right through to Revelation. Covenant meals and meals of fellowship are frequent occurrences in Scripture. Our Shepherd, the Lord Jesus, has given many examples of His open invitation for us to be replenished and restored, to remember and to rejoice at His table. Isaiah 55:1-3 says:

Ho, every one that thirsteth, come ye to the waters, and he that hath no money; come ye, buy, and eat; yea, come, buy wine and milk without money and without price. Wherefore do ye spend money for that which is not bread? and your labor for that which satisfieth not? hearken diligently unto me, and eat ye that which is good, and let your soul delight itself in fatness. Incline your ear, and come unto me; hear, and your soul shall live; and I will make an everlasting covenant with you, even the sure mercies of David.

A table of replenishment. Jesus prepares a table of replenishment when the enemy attacks us with the lie of inadequacy. And I'm not simply referring to our physical needs, but also to our emotional and spiritual needs. Countless times the Lord has graciously prepared a table of replenishment for me when I have felt inadequate for the job and thought I was running out of resources.

It is this unbelievable, supernatural replenishment that awakens the world to see the mighty power of God. Jesus demonstrated, once with a crowd of 5,000 and again with a crowd of 4,000, that He is the God who provides (Matthew

14:14-21; 15:32-38). When the most "responsible" thing to do, in human terms, was to ask the multitudes to find their own food, Jesus turned to the supernatural power of God to provide. Moved with compassion, He confidently told the disciples to begin feeding the multitudes. Jesus did not waver in His complete and utter trust in Jehovah-Jireh.

What is it about your life that you cannot explain apart from God? That's the part of your life that makes the Gospel believable. Let me illustrate. If your neighbor can explain everything about you, then you are just like him—except you're religious. But when he sees God supernaturally meeting your needs, then he will sit up and take notice.

A table of restoration. The most prestigious invitation you will ever receive is the one issued by Jesus: "Come and dine." The invitation is not written on fine linen with embossed lettering. It's written in His blood on a garment of pure, white holiness.

Peter humbly responded to this invitation and dined at the table of restoration. On the night of Jesus' arrest in the Garden of Gethsemane, Peter fled in fear, then denied any knowledge of Jesus three times! In spite of Peter's lack of loyalty, Jesus extended an invitation of mercy to him and said, "Come and dine" (John 21:12). There on the shores of the Sea of Galilee after His resurrection, Jesus came to Peter and prepared a table of restoration (John 21:4-13).

Can you imagine what was going through Peter's mind? Guilt and gladness, fear and fascination, wonder and worship—a kaleidoscope of emotions! He could not believe that he was being invited to the table of the One he had deserted just a short time before. And he was not only invited—he was restored!

The depth of Jesus' covenant love is not exhausted when we sin. There is always forgiveness and restoration at His table.

A table of remembrance. Scripture exhorts us to regularly gather in celebration of the Lord's Supper "till he come" (1 Corinthians 11:23-26). At this most precious of tables, Jesus is not only the host, but the meal. "Whoso eateth my flesh, and drinketh my blood, hath eternal life. . . . For my flesh is meat indeed, and my blood is drink indeed. He that eateth my flesh, and drinketh my blood, dwelleth in me, and I in him" (John 6:54, 56). As by faith we receive Christ's death for us, His substitutionary death on our behalf, we receive eternal life and begin to enjoy an eternal spiritual feast. This is memorialized as often we participate in the precious sacrament of the Lord's Supper.

I must say, nothing satisfies my hunger and thirst more than a meal at the Lord's Table. It is in remembering the blood He shed and the body that was broken that my spirit overflows in gratitude and humility. Thank God we can sit down and feast at the table He has prepared for us.

A table of rejoicing. The best table is yet to come! During Jesus' last supper with His disciples, He said, "For this is my blood of the new testament, which is shed for many for the remission of sins. But I say unto you, I will not drink henceforth of this fruit of the vine, until that day when I drink it new with you in my Father's kingdom" (Matthew 26:28-29).

Where is that going to be? At the marriage supper of the Lamb, a never-ending time of fellowship and rejoicing with Him. There will be no fear of approaching this table unworthily, for we will be not only invited but cleansed for this glorious meal by the Lamb Himself:

Let us be glad and rejoice, and give honor to him: for the marriage of the Lamb is come, and his wife hath made herself ready. And to her was granted that she should be arrayed in fine linen, clean and white: for the fine linen is the righteousness of saints. And he saith unto me, Write, Blessed are they which are called unto the marriage supper of the Lamb.
—REVELATION 19:7-9

There is fullness at the table of the Lord—a table to which He has given His sacrificial attention, so that every place is set and every child is invited. There a greater fullness will be experienced than we've ever known before. This feast will satisfy the deepest hungers of our hearts and the deepest longings of our soul.

Our Shepherd
Freshens Our Spirit

Shepherds used oil to anoint the heads of their sheep to help rid them of nagging pests such as flies. The oil was also used to heal their wounds. Without such an application, the sheep would be frantic, frustrated, and solely focused on getting relief. But with the application of the soothing oil, the sheep were refreshed and able to once again peacefully graze and rest.

Oil was also used as a sign of welcome for an honored guest. In many homes there was a cruse of oil at the front door. As a long-awaited or dearly loved guest would arrive, the host would anoint the head, face, and hair of the guest. The sweet perfume would bring refreshment to the guest, who had usually traveled over dusty roads to reach the host's home.

A fresh anointing. "But my horn shalt thou exalt like the horn of a unicorn: I shall be anointed with fresh oil" (Psalm 92:10). The mercies of the Shepherd in caring for his sheep is a constant reminder of our Lord's caring presence in our lives. We are never anointed by Him with oil that is old or stale or that has lost its fragrance. The oil of His gladness and of His anointing is fresh every day.

The oil of our Lord is like the oil in the widow's jar. When Elijah asked her to bring him a piece of bread, she replied that she had no bread, but only a little flour and a little oil in a jar.

And Elijah said unto her, Fear not; go and do as thou hast said: but make me thereof a little cake first, and bring it unto me, and after make for thee and for thy son. For thus saith the LORD God of Israel, The barrel of meal shall not waste, neither shall the cruse of oil fail, until the day that the LORD sendeth rain upon the earth. And she went and did according to the saying of Elijah: and she, and he, and her house, did eat many days. And the barrel of meal wasted not, neither did the cruse of oil fail, according to the word of the LORD, which he spake by Elijah.
—1 KINGS 17:13-16

The Lord always has more oil for us. The cruse may appear nearly empty to you and to me, but there is always enough for His purposes and for our needs. Like the widow, we only need the Lord's anointing for one day at a time.

Do you experience the fresh anointing of the Lord every morning? If not, I invite you to refresh yourself in prayer, in meditation, and in the reading of His Word first thing in the morning. Such a practice will refresh your soul, heart, and mind better than any cold glass of orange juice or splash of cold water on your face. Oh, how I praise God for His fresh anointing each day. "It is of the LORD's mercies that we are not consumed, because his compassions fail not. They are new every morning: great is thy faithfulness" (Lamentations 3:22-23).

The oil of gladness. Not only is the Lord's oil refreshing—it brings joy to our hearts! When we love what He loves and hate what He hates, He anoints us with the oil of gladness. A happy heart is from God!

Thou lovest righteousness, and hatest wickedness: therefore God, thy God, hath anointed thee with the oil of gladness above thy fellows. All thy garments smell of myrrh, and aloes, and cassia, out of the ivory palaces, whereby they have made thee glad.
—PSALM 45:7-8

When one honored by the Lord comes into His presence as a welcomed guest, the Lord's anointing remains throughout the visit and beyond. All our garments—our very being—then manifest the fragrance of having been in His presence. And that aroma attracts others to our gracious host, the Good Shepherd.

Now thanks be unto God, which always causeth us to triumph in Christ, and maketh manifest the savor of his knowledge by us in every place. For we are unto God a sweet savor of Christ, in them that are saved, and in them that perish: to the one we are the savor of death unto death; and to the other, the savor of life unto life. . . .
—2 CORINTHIANS 2:14-16

Do people smell the sweet fragrance of Christ in your life? I pray that they do. I thank God for the fresh oil of gladness He anoints us with daily. Everything gets stale and old these days. Things wear out with time. But not Jesus. He gets sweeter and more precious with each passing day. His mercies make our hearts glad. When we meditate on His grace, we can't help but want to praise His name!

The oil of the Holy Spirit. Under the New Covenant, we are anointed with the Holy Spirit of God. "Now he which stablisheth us with you in Christ, and hath anointed us, is God; who hath also sealed us, and given the earnest of the Spirit in our hearts" (2 Corinthians 1:21-22).

The anointing of the Holy Spirit seals your salvation. How can you be sure? Just look for the evidence. The fragrance of the Shepherd's presence is none other than the fruit of the Spirit. "But the fruit of the Spirit is love, joy, peace, long-suffering, gentleness, goodness, faith, meekness, temperance" (Galatians 5:22-23).

Whenever peace enters your heart in the midst of grief—whenever joy enters your heart in the midst of a trial—whenever you see evidence of His life in yours, you can be sure the Holy Spirit is flowing through your life with His oil of gladness!

Jesus called the Holy Spirit the Comforter: "But the Comforter, which is the Holy Ghost, whom the Father will send in my name, he shall teach you all things, and bring all things to your remembrance, whatsoever I have said unto you" (John 14:26). Can our Great Shepherd forget us? Never.

The seal of the Holy Spirit, the Comforter, is on our lives, and His oil of gladness sends a sweet aroma of Christ through us to others!

OUR SHEPHERD
FREES OUR SERVICE

The fullest New Testament revelation of Jesus Christ as our Shepherd is in the Gospel of John, chapter 10. There we see, in His own words, the abundance of the life He gives us:

The thief cometh not, but for to steal, and to kill, and to destroy: I am come that they might have life, and that they might have it more abundantly. I am the good shepherd: the good shepherd giveth his life for the sheep.

—JOHN 10:10-11

The Good Shepherd exchanged the abundance of His life for the abundance of our sin, in order that our cups might overflow. He doesn't just give us life—a cup half full—then send us on our way; He gives us *abundant* life, a cup overflowing for all eternity! Paul explains that Jesus

being in the form of God, thought it not robbery to be equal with God: but made himself of no reputation, and took upon him the form of a servant, and was made in the likeness of men: and being found in fashion as a man, he humbled himself, and became obedient unto death, even the death of the cross.

—PHILIPPIANS 2:6-8

Immediately preceding this description, Paul exhorts us to have this same servant attitude. God's gift of love through His Son Jesus Christ liberates us to serve Him with grateful hearts. God is the God of the open hand and the open heart. How freely He gives. In Matthew 10:8 Jesus says, ". . . freely ye have received, freely give."

Do you know what Bible scholars tell us about the amount of wine Jesus made from water (John 2)? One hundred and twenty gallons! Their cups overflowed! And when Jesus fed 5,000 men plus women and children with a few loaves and fishes, there were twelve baskets left over! Their cup ran over too!

Do you know what some people want to do when their cup begins to over-flow? They want a bigger cup! We don't need a bigger cup—we need to share the love that is flowing through us with our neighbor who needs to hear about Jesus. We need to pour forth His love to the hurting saint in our church who needs His encouragement. Let your cup run over and be a blessing to somebody else. Jesus exhorts us, "for out of the abundance of the heart the mouth speaketh" (Matthew 12:34). We have the awesome privilege of letting our Shepherd's love reach flood tide in our hearts, then pour out to those around us!

What do we have in Jesus? Love overflowing. We have fullness in Christ. We have freshness in Christ. We have freeness in Christ. The beautiful refrain of the hymn "He Giveth More Grace" by Annie Johnson Flint says:

His love has no limit,
His grace has no measure,
His pow'r has no boundary known unto men;
For out of his infinite riches in Jesus,
He giveth and giveth and giveth again.

Don't let the devil corrupt your thinking about God. Stay true to the Good News. He has prepared a table for you. Come and dine.

The King of Love My Shepherd Is

The King of love my Shepherd is,
Whose goodness faileth never;
I nothing lack if I am his,
And he is mine forever.

Where streams of living water flow,
My Ransomed soul he leadeth,
And, where the verdant pastures grow,
With food celestial feedeth.

Perverse and foolish, oft I strayed,
But yet in love he sought me,
And on his shoulder gently laid,
And home, rejoicing, brought me.

In death's dark vale I fear no ill,
With thee, dear Lord, beside me;
Thy rod and staff my comfort still,
Thy cross before to guide me.

And so through all the length of days,
Thy goodness faileth never;
Good Shepherd, may I sing thy praise,
Within thy house for ever. Amen.

93

CHAPTER SIX

THE SHEPHERD OF HEAVEN

The sure provisions of my God

Attend me all my days;

O may Thy house be my abode,

And all my work be praise.

There would I find a settled rest,

While others go and come;

No more a stranger, nor a guest,

But like a child at home.

ISAAC WATTS

*A*re you familiar with the phrase "he saved the best for last" or "the best is yet to come"? Despite all of Satan's hype about the enticing things he offers, he always gives the best first and the worst last.

Proverbs 20:17 says, "Bread of deceit is sweet to a man; but afterwards his mouth shall be filled with gravel." Satan will tempt us with delicacies, riches, power, fame, and popularity, but in the end they will bite us with flaming fervor. Satan doesn't give us the full story when he tempts us. He is the chief counterfeiter and is always guilty of false advertising. His temptations taste sweet for the moment, but ultimately, God's Word says, that sweetness will turn sour. Gravel instead of strawberries. Not a tasty end to what started out as a delicious temptation.

Satan tries every angle to get our eyes off the eternal hope of glory and onto the temporal happiness of self-gratification. Satan will say, "Get all you can keep. Keep all you can get. Eat, drink, and be merry, for tomorrow you may die. Don't worry about the future. You only go around once in life, so grab all you can!"

Even many television commercials try to spread this lie. In one, a group of men sit around a campfire enjoying a time of camaraderie. One of them lifts a beer and toasts his friends, saying, "It doesn't get any better than this!" And he's right. It only gets worse!

Wouldn't it be interesting if the same advertiser showed these men drinking their beer while talking about the long-term effects of alcohol? The thousands of lives lost annually due to alcohol-related car accidents. The neglect of children due to alcoholic mothers and fathers. The millions of medical dollars and jobs lost to alcoholism. I don't think this will be a campaign we'll be seeing anytime soon. Satan doesn't want the truth to be told.

But God is just the opposite of Satan. His Word tells us that He has "begotten us again unto a lively hope by the resurrection of Jesus Christ from the dead, to an inheritance incorruptible, and undefiled, and that fadeth not away, reserved in heaven for you" (1 Peter 1:3-4). If you are a child of God, you have a standing reservation in heaven! And it really doesn't get any better than that!

The best is yet to be! This doesn't mean that what we currently receive from God is bad—but what is to come is even better. But by God's grace, in spite of a sin-wrecked world, we can enjoy life immensely even now. So much joy and beauty can be ours daily. Psalm 68:19 says, "Blessed be the LORD, who daily loadeth us with benefits, even the God of our salvation."

Jesus gives us the best last. Remember the marriage celebration recorded in John 2:1-10 when Jesus changed the water into wine? The master of ceremonies came to Him and couldn't understand why the best wine was served last. That's Jesus. He keeps getting better and better. As the hymn writer said, "Every day with Jesus is sweeter than the day before." The longer you are a Christian, the sweeter your relationship with your Savior grows.

If you know Jesus, goodness and mercy will pursue you all

the days of your life. That's what the word "follow" literally means in this passage—pursue. Jesus pursued you with His call of salvation. He will continue to pursue you throughout your life, surrounding you with His goodness and mercy. These two attributes of our Shepherd are like two sheep dogs that follow the flock to make sure they have a safe journey to the desired destination.

Have you ever questioned God's provision in your life and wondered if He really cared for you? So have I. But there is no question about His love for us. "Surely," David says, not "hopefully." It is certain. God promises that His goodness and mercy will always find us.

Dr. Harry Ironside, former pastor of Moody Memorial Church in Chicago, told a story that went something like this:

There was a poor, dear lady who lived by herself. She was haunted by fear, including a phobia that she thought two men were following her everywhere she went. She came to see her pastor about it.

"Pastor, I have a very serious problem."

"What is it?"

She said, "Everywhere I go, two men follow me. When I go to the grocery store, they follow me. When I get on the streetcar, they get on too. When I come home, they're right behind me."

He asked, "Have you reported this to the police?"

She said, "Yes, but they say they're not there. But I know they are. Always."

With compassion in his voice, he said, "Oh, you are a most blessed woman. Don't you know who these men are?"

She said, "No. Do you?"

He said, "Oh yes. They're David's friends."

Then he turned to Psalm 23 and read it to his distressed parishioner, ending with the words, "Surely goodness and mercy shall follow me all the days of my life." Then he said, "Those two men are goodness and mercy. And God has sent them to follow you all the days of your life."

She said, "Pastor, that's wonderful. And to think all this time, I've been afraid of them."

From that day on, she would go to the streetcar and wait for goodness and mercy to get on with her. When she'd come home to her apartment, she'd open the door and let goodness and mercy go in. She lived the rest of her life this way until she stepped over to the other side and her new home of perfect happiness and peace.

The story is somewhat whimsical, but the truth it illustrates is true and precious. Oh, that we could understand in a very real way that God's goodness and mercy will follow us all the days of our lives! His goodness in the good times of our lives—provision, healing, guidance. His mercy in the lean times of our lives—correction, forgiveness, compassion, understanding. God's goodness and mercy will attend us wherever we go for the rest of our lives. Yes, sometimes you and I will stumble. But in His goodness and mercy He will pick us up and set us on our feet again.

The fact that these words immediately follow the phrase "my cup runneth over" is particularly important. Out of the fullness of our cup, thanks to His goodness and mercy, we are able to give, give, and give some more. Jesus promised, "Give, and it shall be given unto you; good measure, pressed down, and shaken together, and running over" (Luke 6:38). We give because our cup runs over. We must not sit, soak, and grow sour with the blessings we have received. We give and keep giving!

As surely as the sun rises and sets, God will pursue us with His goodness and mercy all the days of our lives! Not because we deserve it, but because He loves us!

The Certainty of Heaven

David's declaration of heaven is with total assurance. He doesn't say, "I might dwell," or "I hope to dwell," but "I will dwell." It's as if he is giving us an outline of the places where he would live during his lifetime on earth. "As a small lad, I lived in Bethlehem. When I was a young man, I hid from Saul in the Judean wilderness. As a king, I will reign in Jerusalem. And when I die, I will go to live with my Lord."

Heaven is a real place. Jesus confirmed this truth when He said:

Let not your heart be troubled: ye believe in God, believe also in me. In my Father's house are many mansions: if it were not so, I would have told you. I go to prepare a place for you. And if I go and prepare a place for you, I will come again, and receive you unto myself; that where I am, there ye may be also.

—JOHN 14:1-3

Do you believe that Jesus is "the way, the truth, and the life," as He said in John 14:6? If He is "the truth" (and He is), He wouldn't lie about your mansion in heaven. Heaven is as real as the home or apartment or whatever you are living in right now. Heaven is not merely a state of mind. How can it be merely a place you can retreat to in your mind if Jesus is living there in a real body—fully man and yet fully God? What kind of Lord would deceive His children by building up their hope of a better day if that day was not coming?

Furthermore, Paul said that on one occasion he was caught up into the third heaven:

I knew a man in Christ above fourteen years ago, (whether in the body, I cannot tell; or whether out of the body, I cannot tell: God knoweth;) such a one caught up to the third heaven. And I knew such a man, (whether in the body, or out of the body, I cannot tell: God knoweth;) how that he was caught up into paradise, and heard unspeakable words, which it is not lawful for a man to utter.

—2 CORINTHIANS 12:2-4

Where is "the third heaven"? The Bible is not perfectly clear on this, but it must be in a different place than some of the "heavens" referred to elsewhere in Scripture. There is a heaven where the birds fly (Genesis 1:20). There is a heaven in which the moon, sun, stars, and planets exist (Deuteronomy 4:19). And there is the third heaven to which Paul was taken.

As has been so beautifully said, "We see the first heaven by day, the second heaven by night, and the third heaven by faith." Heaven is not accepted on blind faith. It is part of the truth revealed by the One we embrace, the Lord of heaven Himself. It was Paul who reminded us that "whilst we are at home in the body, we are absent from the Lord: (for we walk by faith, not by sight)" (2 Corinthians 5:6-7).

Heaven is a present place. When a believer dies, he or she steps right into heaven. "Verily I say unto thee, Today shalt thou be with me [Jesus] in paradise" (Luke 23:43). Today—not tomorrow, not next year, but today. When you breathe your last breath, you will be with Jesus in paradise!

The first martyr of the Christian faith, Stephen, saw heaven open up during his final seconds of life. Christ had ascended into heaven just a short time earlier, and now Stephen's convicting message enraged the Jewish leadership in Jerusalem:

But he [Stephen], being full of the Holy Ghost, looked up steadfastly into heaven, and saw the glory of God, and Jesus standing on the right hand of God, and said, Behold, I see the heavens opened, and the Son of man standing on the right hand of God.

—ACTS 7:55-56

Can you imagine being on your deathbed, looking up into heaven, and seeing Jesus standing at the right hand of God waiting for your arrival? The sheer joy of that vision strengthened Stephen to withstand the stoning that followed his message. And not only that—the vision enabled him to forgive his tormentors.

Calling out to God, he said, "Lord Jesus, receive my spirit. And he kneeled down, and cried with a loud voice, Lord, lay not this sin to their charge. And when he had said this, he fell asleep" (Acts 7:59-60). *Asleep.* I wonder if any of us could fall asleep while someone was stoning us to death! Whether this phrase is literal or is simply a figurative expression for death, that is exactly the kind of peace we will receive when we see our Savior face to face!

Heaven is a perfect place. Revelation 21:4 says, "And God shall wipe away all tears from their eyes; and there shall be no more death, neither sorrow, nor crying, neither shall there be any more pain: for the former things are passed away." We will be in the very presence of all that is good and will celebrate the absence of all that is evil. Perfection. No more doubts. No more fears.

Not only is heaven perfect in the sense of God's presence being there, but it will be perfect in His provision. Heaven is going to be all that the loving heart of God can conceive and that the omnipotent hand of God can prepare. Think of how a perfect shepherd would provide for his sheep! He would do everything in his power to provide the best he possibly could. Now multiply that by infinity! We'd better start preparing for something pretty special!

Heaven is a purposeful place. If you're thinking heaven is a place where you'll snack on bonbons all day on a fluffy cloud while strumming a harp, I'm afraid you've confused what the Bible has to say with the comic-strip version of heaven. Revelation 7:15-17 says:

Therefore are they before the throne of God, and serve him day and night in his temple: and he that sitteth on the throne shall dwell among them. They shall hunger no more, neither thirst any more; neither shall the sun light on them, nor any heat. For the Lamb which is in the midst of the throne shall feed them, and shall lead them unto living fountains of waters: and God shall wipe away all tears from their eyes.

I suppose that every Christian singer wishes he or she could sing with more fervor and more beauty in order to give God greater glory. I imagine every person who serves the widow and orphan in need wishes he or she could serve tirelessly and with greater passion. One day, when our sinful flesh is no longer holding us down, we will serve Him as never before!

Imagine the choir of angels we will hear around the throne of Jesus Christ! Revelation 5:11 says, "The number of them was ten thousand times ten thousand, and thousands of thousands." Over one hundred million voices singing in perfect harmony in praise of our Great God! What a joyous noise they will be making to the Lord! And yet you are not just one in a hundred million. He loves you as an individual, and He knows your name.

THE COMPANY OF HEAVEN.
Not only are believers certain that heaven exists, but we are certain that we are going to live forever in the household of the Lord. In fact, every child of God is already a member of that household. Paul says:

Now therefore ye are no more strangers and foreigners, but fellow citizens with the saints, and of the household of God; and are built upon the foundation of the apostles and prophets, Jesus Christ himself being the chief corner stone; in whom all the building fitly framed together groweth unto a holy temple in the Lord: in whom ye also are builded together for an habitation of God through the Spirit.
—EPHESIANS 2:19-22

We will one day be in the presence of God surrounded by the hosts of heaven and the saints of old. Everyone in the household of the faith will be there. Moses will be there. David will be there. Paul. Jacob. Mary, the mother of Jesus. Abraham. Esther. Ruth. All the saints you've heard about and some you've never heard about. They will all be there. Imagine sitting down for a few centuries and listening to these brothers and sisters talk about God's faithfulness and grace. What a grand homecoming that will be!

People ask me, "Will I see my loved ones in heaven?" Yes, those who knew Jesus. In fact, that will be the only place we will ever truly know them. Both they, and we, will be changed forever. We will, in character, become like the only three perfect people who ever walked the face of the earth—the first Adam and his wife (before their sin), and the last Adam, Jesus As a matter of fact we gain more in Jesus than we ever lost in Adam. Adam was innocent before he sinned. The redeemed have the imputed righteousness of Jesus. I had rather be a saved sinner than innocent Adam (see 1 Corinthians 15:45)!

One of the most poignant pictures of this reunion is found in David's life. He and Bathsheba had a child as a result of their adulterous relationship. Part of God's judgment upon David and his household was that this child would not live. When the child became sick shortly after childbirth, the Bible says, "David therefore besought God for the child; and David fasted, and went in, and lay all night upon the earth. And the elders of his house arose, and went to him, to raise him up from the earth: but he would not, neither did he eat bread with them" (2 Samuel 12:16-17). And just as God said, the child passed away shortly thereafter.

Instead of mourning, "David arose from the earth, and washed, and anointed himself, and changed his apparel, and came into the house of the LORD, and worshipped: then he came to his own house; and when he required, they set bread before him, and he did eat" (verse 20). His servants couldn't believe David's response, but he said, "Can I bring him back again? I shall go to him, but he shall not return to me" (verse 23). David knew that one day he would be with his child again, and he took comfort in that fact.

Do you have a little baby in heaven? Joyce and I have a little boy waiting to see us there. His name is Philip, and we're going to see him again. Some may call this sheer sentimentality. We call it believing the Bible. When I think of a baby going to heaven, I'm reminded of the following story about a shepherd and his little lamb.

There was a shepherd who had led his flock to a cold, turbulent stream. He knew they had to cross to the other side, but the sheep were afraid. With great care and divine wisdom, the shepherd picked up a little lamb, put it in his arms, and waded across the chilly waters. Setting the lamb down on the other side, he turned to see that the lamb's ewe and ram had come to the stream's edge. Their eyes were fixed on their lamb. It didn't take long before the ewe and ram started across the water. Moments later the entire flock followed.

Sometimes our Father takes a little lamb from among our flock as well. We can't understand our loss because we cannot comprehend the mysteries of God. But one thing we know—

He knows what is best for each one of His children. And He has prepared a place for each one—a place of perfect peace and joy. Praise God—we will meet our loved ones there.

We will "dwell in the house of the LORD for ever." That is the best news yet. Certainly we will be overjoyed to be reunited with our loved ones, but how much greater will be our joy at spending time with Jesus! To see Him face to face. To sit at His feet. To listen to His voice. To feel His touch. Oh, what joy unspeakable! And not just for a moment, but for all eternity!

THE CONSTANCY OF HEAVEN

Forever. This word had a precious meaning to shepherds who lived seminomadic lifestyles, moving with their flock to wherever pastures were green and waters were still. Their temporary homes were simply sheepfolds. When the grass withered and the water became muddy, they would pack up, move out, and travel on. Without question, this nomadic existence was a trial.

The wandering of the shepherd is a helpful picture of the life of believers on earth. This world is not our home. We are simply passing through as messengers and ambassadors of the Good News of Jesus Christ. If you sometimes feel out of place, without roots, detached for whatever reason, take heart—that's how homesickness feels! Your Chief Shepherd is preparing a permanent home for you in heaven, and he is waiting to see you there!

There are many wonderful things about this world that I

have grown quite accustomed to, but I often remind myself that they in no way compare to the riches of heaven. If you find yourself growing comfortable with your home in this world, remember: Satan always puts out the best first and the worst last! Your home is over there, not over here. Your destiny is forever, not wherever. Let's put our trust in the Shepherd who saves the best for last! What a glorious revelation is the certainty of heaven, the company of heaven, and the constancy of heaven!

Psalm 23 is all about Jesus—His sufficiency, His supremacy, His sovereignty! It is all Him. He is all we need. Seek Him with all your heart, soul, and mind and you will never want for anything. Your deepest longings will be met in the Shepherd, the Lord Jesus Christ.

The psalmist's words elsewhere are my prayer for you: "O give thanks unto the LORD; call upon his name: make known his deeds among the people. Sing unto him, sing psalms unto him: talk ye of all his wondrous works. Glory ye in his holy name: let the heart of them rejoice that seek the LORD. Seek the LORD, and his strength: seek his face evermore" (Psalm 105:1-4).

I heard a story about a godly woman who loved the Lord with all her heart. In her later years she began losing her memory. Details about everyday life seem to fade. Even names of her family began to elude her. And finally even the faces of her loved ones slipped from her recollection.

Throughout her life she treasured the Word of God, memorizing many texts from her threadbare Bible. Her favorite verse had always been 2 Timothy 1:12, which says, "For I know whom I have believed, and am persuaded that he is able to keep that which I have committed unto him against that day."

As her memory worsened and her body became more and more weak, her family decided she should live out her final days in the care of a nursing home. Her family came often for visits, and each time she would quote her favorite verses, including the passage from 2 Timothy.

Weeks passed, and though her love for Jesus never waned, her body weakened and her voice became faint. As she was dying, her family could still hear her repeating 2 Timothy 1:12, but the words became fewer and fewer. At the end there was only word left she could say: "Him."

She whispered it again and again with her dying breath. "Him . . . Him . . . Him." It was all she could say and all she had left. She held on to the word that was closest to her heart and indeed the word that is at the heart of His own Word: "Him".

He is all you need. He is all I need. The secret to peace is Jesus. The secret to joy is Jesus. The secret to satisfaction is Jesus. The Lord is our Shepherd—we shall not want.

Face to Face

Face to face with Christ my Savior, Face to face—what will it be—
When with rapture I behold Him, Jesus Christ who died for me?

> *Chorus:*
> *Face to face I shall behold Him, Far beyond the starry sky;*
> *Face to face in all His glory, I shall see Him by and by!*

Only faintly now I see Him, With the darkened veil between,
But a blessed day is coming, When His glory shall be seen.

What rejoicing in His presence, When are banished grief and pain,
When the crooked ways are straightened, And the dark things shall be plain.

Face to face! O blissful moment! Face to face—to see and know;
Face to face with my Redeemer, Jesus Christ who loves me so.